Our
Michigan

Voyageur Press

First published in 2004 by Voyageur Press an imprint of MBI Publishing Company LLC, Galtier Plaza, Suite 200, 380 Jackson Street, St. Paul, MN 55101 USA

MBI Publishing Company titles are also available at discounts in bulk quantity for industrial or sales-promotional use. For details write to Special Sales Manager at MBI Publishing Company, Galtier Plaza, Suite 200, 380 Jackson Street, St. Paul, MN 55101 USA.

To find out more about our books, join us online at www. voyageurpress.com.

Library of Congress Cataloging-in-Publication Data

Our Michigan / edited by Margret Aldrich.
    p. cm.
ISBN-13: 978-0-89658-043-5 (hardcover)
ISBN-10: 0-89658-043-1 (hardcover)
1. Michigan—Pictorial works. I. Aldrich, Margret, 1975–
F567.O97 2004
977.4'022'2—dc22

                    2003018754

Edited by Margret Aldrich
Printed in Hong Kong

Page 1: *A solitary fisherman contemplates the sunset over Lake Superior. (Photograph © Terry Donnelly)*

Page 2: *The shoreline is rippled with golden sand formations at Pictured Rocks National Lakeshore on Michigan's Upper Peninsula. (Photograph © Doug Locke)*

Page 3, top: *Two boys leap off of a dock into the sparkling waters of Wamplers Lake, found in the Irish Hills region of southeastern Michigan. (Photograph © Keith Baum/Baums-Away Stock Photography)*

Page 3, bottom: *Mackinac Island, located between the state's Upper and Lower peninsulas, is a popular destination for Michiganders and tourists alike. (Photograph © Layne Kennedy)*

Page 4: *The Renaissance Center stands tall at the edge of downtown Detroit. The central tower is seventy-three stories high. (Photograph © Keith Baum/BaumsAway Stock Photography)*

Page 5: *Every summer, the Michigan Challenge Balloonfest draws a crowd to the small town of Howell, where the sky overhead is filled with colorful hot-air balloons. (Photograph © Keith Baum/BaumsAway Stock Photography)*

Title page: *Lake of the Clouds, in the Carp River Valley, is surrounded by the autumnal hues of the Porcupine Mountains Wilderness State Park. (Photograph © Terry Donnelly)*

Title page inset: *The colors of fall are reflected on the shimmering waters of the Presque Isle River. (Photograph © Terry Donnelly)*

Facing page: *The holes in this mighty pine tree, which grows beside the Presque Isle River Trail, are evidence of a woodpecker. (Photograph © Layne Kennedy)*

Facing page: *Big Carp River meanders through the hardwood forest of the Upper Peninsula's Porcupine Mountains. (Photograph © Terry Donnelly)*

Above: *The four-mile Escarpment Trail offers hikers some of the most beautiful views of Porcupine Mountains Wilderness State Park. (Photograph © Layne Kennedy)*

Small, dark pools form below Manido Falls in Porcupine Mountains Wilderness State Park. (Photograph © Willard Clay)

Leaves and pine needles collect in the crevices of these black, water-sculpted rocks. (Photograph © Terry Donnelly)

Left: *Stone slabs and birch trees at the edge of Porcupine Mountains Wilderness State Park glow with the warm shades of autumn. (Photograph © Gary Alan Nelson)*

Above: *Rain droplets dot fallen maple leaves. (Photograph © Doug Locke)*

Right: *Against a dusk-painted sky, backpackers trek along the beach. (Photograph © Layne Kennedy)*

Below: *Manistee Lighthouse stands watch over Lake Michigan at sunset. (Photograph © Gary Alan Nelson)*

Facing page: *Breaking ice floats at the edge of Lake Michigan, where the water meets Sleeping Bear Dunes National Lakeshore. (Photograph © Gary Alan Nelson)*

Evening light illuminates the dune grasses and white-sand beach of Good Harbor Bay. Pyramid Point and Sleeping Bear Dunes are seen on the horizon. (Photograph © Mary Liz Austin)

The steel Frankfort North Breakwater Light of Benzie County was erected in 1932. (Photograph © Terry Donnelly)

With over 3,200 miles of shoreline and 11,000 inland lakes, Michigan is a haven for boaters. (Photograph © Gary Alan Nelson)

Nets hang like gossamer on a boat at Leeland. Ferries travel between the historic town and the Manitou Islands. (Photograph © Layne Kennedy)

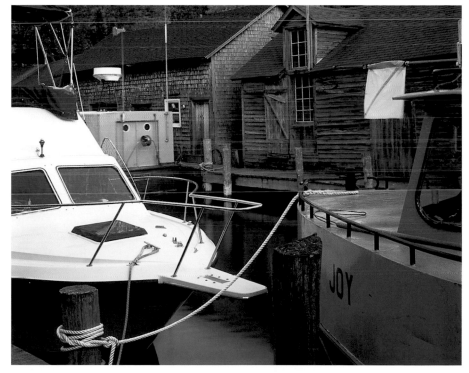

Weathered, gray buildings are clustered together at Fishtown, a section of Leland on Northwest Michigan's thirty-five-mile-long Leelanau Peninsula. (Photograph © Terry Donnelly)

On a sunny, summer day, the 71,000-acre Sleeping Bear Dunes National Lakeshore stretches as far as the eye can see. (Photograph © Mary Liz Austin)

23

Hoary puccoon stubbornly sprouts from the sand of Sleeping Bear Dunes. The dunes are 460 feet tall in some areas. (Photograph © Terry Donnelly)

Tree branches are tossed by a Lake Michigan breeze. (Photograph © Layne Kennedy)

The Sleeping Bear Point Lifesaving Station was established in 1901 in an effort to rescue passengers and crewmembers of shipwrecked barges traveling the Manitou Passage. (Photograph © Terry Donnelly)

Michigan is the third-largest producer of apples in the United States, ranked behind only Washington and New York. (Photograph © Layne Kennedy)

Sutton's Bay, located on the coast of Grand Traverse Bay, boasts a charming downtown area where streets are lined with shops and restaurants. (Photograph © Layne Kennedy)

Petoskey's Gaslight District offers a variety of locally owned stores and boutiques to explore. (Photograph © Layne Kennedy)

Every summer, Traverse City hosts "Boats on the Boardwalk," a display of classic watercraft. (Photograph © Jim Allor)

Traverse City, founded in the 1870s, thrives as a close-knit community and tourist destination, with ample opportunities for sightseeing and shopping. (Photograph © Layne Kennedy)

Each July, the National Cherry Festival is held in Traverse City, known as the "Cherry Capital of the World." (Photograph © Jim Allor)

Left: *A red schoolhouse decorated with Christmas wreaths stands in contrast to the white, fresh-fallen snow. (Photo graph © Terry Donnelly)*

Above: *At the edge of the Manistee National Forest, near Cadillac, a group of delighted passengers enjoy a horse-drawn sleigh ride. (Photograph © Richard Hirneisen Photography)*

Above: *Eighteen miles north of Traverse City on Grand Traverse Bay's Old Mission Peninsula stands the Old Mission Point Light, built in 1870. (Photograph © Keith Baum/ BaumsAway Stock Photography)*

Right: *The late-afternoon sun warms the frozen shoreline of Lake Michigan and the maize-colored grasses of Muskegon State Park. (Photograph © Terry Donnelly)*

Facing page: *White birch trees rise from the snow-covered ground of the Nordhouse Dunes Wilderness Area, a 1,900-acre preserve in the Manistee National Forest. (Photograph © Terry Donnelly)*

Above: *In Ludington State Park, a hiking trail leads to Big Sable Point Light. The Big Sable Lighthouse Keeper's Association works to keep the 1867 structure in prime condition. (Photograph © Layne Kennedy)*

There are over 52,000 farms in Michigan, whose top exports include soybeans, fruits, vegetables, and livestock. (Photograph © Richard Hirneisen Photography)

Above: *With 13,500 acres of vineyards, Michigan is the fourth-largest grape-growing state. (Photograph © Keith Baum/BaumsAway Stock Photography)*

Right: *A weathered barn and grassy pasture in rural Osceola County complete this pastoral scene. (Photograph © Gary Alan Nelson)*

Kellogg's Cereal City USA informs visitors that breakfast cereal was born in Battle Creek in 1906, when Will Keith Kellogg founded the Battle Creek Toasted Corn Flake Company. (Photograph © Keith Baum/BaumsAway Stock Photography)

Above: *The Pere Marquette #1223 locomotive, found at the Tri-Cities Historical Museum, is an artifact of steam-operated railroads' glory days. (Photograph © Layne Kennedy)*

Facing page: *Pieces of everyday life from Victorian-era Michigan can be found at the Tri-Cities Historical Museum in Grand Haven. (Photograph © Layne Kennedy)*

Fishing boats patrol the water surrounding Grand Haven's Inner and Outer Lights. (Photograph © Keith Baum/BaumsAway Stock Photography)

The Frederik Meijer Gardens of Grand Rapids is home to a twenty-four-foot-tall bronze statue of a horse, which is a replica of Leonardo da Vinci's original design. (Photograph © Richard Hirneisen Photography)

As the sun sets, a barge moves slowly across Lake Michigan. (Photograph © Layne Kennedy)

Catwalk lights illuminate the horizon at the Grand Haven pier. (Photograph © Terry Donnelly)

Legend has it that after the sawmill town of Singapore was abandoned in the late 1800s, the drifting sand of the Saugatuck Dunes completely buried the site. (Photograph © Layne Kennedy)

Today, the Saugatuck Sand Dunes are a popular recreation area. (Photograph © Layne Kennedy)

Beach grasses whisper in the breeze on the shore of Lake Michigan. (Photograph © Gary Alan Nelson)

At day's end, a boat on Lake Michigan is silhouetted against a peaceful sky. (Photograph © Gary Alan Nelson)

Above: *Brightly painted Holland Harbor Light is affectionately called "Big Red" by the locals. (Photograph © Keith Baum/BaumsAway Stock Photography)*

Facing page: *The Wilhelm Baum, a restored tugboat, is docked at the Michigan Maritime Museum in South Haven. (Photograph © Terry Donnelly)*

In a dramatic display of spray and foam, the waters of Lake Michigan crash into the pier of the South Haven Light. (Photograph © Doug Locke)

Facing page: *Windmills, tulips, and other evidence of Dutch ancestry abound in the town of Holland, which was settled in 1847. (Photograph © Keith Baum/BaumsAway Stock Photography)*

Above: *Wooden clogs, or* klompen, *are worn by parade participants during the ten-day Holland Tulip Time Festival. (Photograph © Layne Kennedy)*

Saugatuck's attractions include art galleries, shops, and historic buildings, like Peterson Mill. (Photograph © Terry Donnelly)

Above: *The Kalamazoo Aviation History Museum, nicknamed the Kalamazoo Air Zoo, houses a flock of fantastic planes, such as the Curtis P-40 Flying Tiger and the Grumman Wildcat. (Photograph © Layne Kennedy)*

Left: *Although Michigan has a population of 9,938,444 people, natural areas are still plentiful. Residents enjoy three national parks and four of the five Great Lakes. (Photograph © Layne Kennedy)*

Right: *When Michigan became a state in 1837, Detroit was named the temporary capital, but ten years later, Lansing was declared permanent capital of the Great Lakes State. (Photograph © Keith Baum/ BaumsAway Stock Photography)*

Below: *Originally dedicated in 1879, the Lansing state capitol building underwent renovations in 1992 to restore both its interior and exterior to their former glory. (Photograph © Keith Baum/BaumsAway Stock Photography)*

The Blue Water Bridge connects the state of Michigan to Canada at Port Huron. (Photograph © Keith Baum/BaumsAway Stock Photography)

Ann Arbor's lively atmosphere and healthy economy are due, in large part, to the presence of the University of Michigan. (Photograph © Keith Baum/BaumsAway Stock Photography)

Pigs race to the finish line at Livonia Spree, an annual festival in Livonia that raises funds to further community development. (Photograph © Keith Baum/BaumsAway Stock Photography)

Right: *Everyone wants to try their luck on the Michigan State Fair midway. First held in 1849, the fair is the oldest in the nation. (Photograph © Jim Allor)*

Facing page: *The Henry Ford Museum in Dearborn houses a vast collection of Americana that documents the ingenuity and creative spirit of the nation's citizens. (Photograph © Layne Kennedy)*

Above: *The Lansing Lugnuts, a Midwest League affiliate of the Chicago Cubs, are cheered on by their mascot "Big Lug" at Oldsmobile Park. (Photograph © Richard Hirneisen Photography)*

Above: *After eighty-seven years of baseball, the Detroit Tigers played their final game at Tiger Stadium on September 27, 1999, and moved to the newly built Comerica Park in 2000. (Photograph © Keith Baum/BaumsAway Stock Photography)*

Right: *Downtown Detroit provides a backdrop for Comerica Park, home of the Tigers. (Photograph © Keith Baum/BaumsAway Stock Photography)*

Above: *The city of Detroit shows its admiration for the Red Wings, their local hockey team, by dressing up the Spirit of Detroit statue in a team jersey. (Photograph © Doug Locke)*

Right: *The Detroit Zoological Institute celebrates animals from around the world, and also works with local conservation programs to protect Michigan's native wildlife. (Photograph © Layne Kennedy)*

Facing page: *In downtown Detroit, the Joe Louis Fist memorializes heavyweight boxing champion Louis, also known as the "Brown Bomber." (Photograph © Keith Baum/ BaumsAway Stock Photography)*

Overleaf: *On the banks of the Detroit River, the city skyline lights up a darkening sky. (Photograph © Gary Alan Nelson)*

Facing page: *The Fox Theater first opened its doors to audiences in 1928 and continues to amaze with its mighty columns and gilded ceiling. (Photograph © Richard Hirneisen Photography)*

Above: *With over 65,000 works in its collection, the Detroit Institute of Arts is one of the largest fine arts museums in the United States. (Photograph © Keith Baum/BaumsAway Stock Photography)*

Left: *Ethnic dancers pose in front of Mexican muralist Diego Rivera's fresco,* Detroit Industry, *at the Institute of Arts. (Photograph © Richard Hirneisen Photography)*

The Woodward Dream Cruise, the world's largest one-day car show, celebrates the Motor City's fascination with automobiles. (Photograph © Richard Hirneisen Photography)

Facing page: *Greektown, where authentic Greek food is served in a bevy of vibrant restaurants, is one of Detroit's most popular dining destinations. (Photograph © Layne Kennedy)*

Left: *Colorful bottles line the shelves of Thomas Edison's laboratory, replicated at the Ford Museum in Greenfield Village. (Photograph © Layne Kennedy)*

The Motown Museum in Detroit immortalizes great acts like the Supremes, the Temptations, and the Jackson 5. (Photograph © Layne Kennedy)

The dazzling fireworks display at the International Freedom Festival in Detroit is one of the largest in the world and attracts more than one million viewers. (Photograph © Keith Baum/ BaumsAway Stock Photography)

Above: *Built in 1908, the Chesaning Heritage House is evidence of the wealth that logging once brought to Saginaw County. (Photograph © Richard Hirneisen Photography)*

Facing page: *The Plymouth International Ice Sculpture Spectacular, North America's oldest and largest ice-carving competition, transforms the town into a winter wonderland each January. (Photograph © Richard Hirneisen Photography)*

Above: *Michigan's parks and natural areas provide ample opportunity for birdwatching. (Photograph © Doug Locke)*

Above: *The Michigan Wildlife Conservancy works to restore native wildlife habitats, so that animals, like the gray wolf, can continue to survive in the state. (Photograph © Doug Locke)*

An ice-encrusted crabapple tree in eastern Michigan glistens after a storm. (Photograph © Claudia Adams)

Facing page: *Leaves burst into intense shades of orange and gold at autumn's debut in Michigan. (Photograph © Robert W. Domm)*

Left: *Three members of the deer family live in Michigan: white-tailed deer, elk, and moose. Whitetails, the smallest of the three, can be found throughout the state. (Photograph © Robert W. Domm)*

Below: *Wash Oak School, in Northville, is one of the last remaining one-room schoolhouses in Michigan. (Photograph © Keith Baum/ BaumsAway Stock Photography)*

Sunflowers nod in a Standish farm field near Saginaw Bay. (Photograph © Doug Locke)

The Mail Pouch Tobacco advertisement on this weathered barn has been faded by years of sun and rain. (Photograph © Claudia Adams)

Crossroads Village, in Flint, lets visitors experience what Michigan life was like in the 1800s. (Photograph © Richard Hirneisen Photography)

Each year, a multitude of visitors travel to the town of Frankenmuth, dubbed "Michigan's Little Bavaria," and cross Zehnder's Wooden Bridge. (Photograph © Keith Baum/BaumsAway Stock Photography)

Carefully hand-stitched Amish Star quilts hang on a line at a Central Michigan roadside stand. (Photograph © Keith Baum/ BaumsAway Stock Photography)

Above: *At the Fort Michilimackinac military reenactment, a soldier stands at attention with his drum. (Photograph © Keith Baum/BaumsAway Stock Photography)*

Historic Fort Michilimackinac was the site of a dramatic, surprise attack during the French and Indian War. (Photograph © Keith Baum/BaumsAway Stock Photography)

Facing page: *North of Harrisville is the Sturgeon Point Lighthouse and Museum, a structure built in 1869 that wears a coat of white with red trim. (Photograph © Terry Donnelly)*

Facing page: *Old Mackinac Point Light, located between Lake Michigan and Lake Huron, was active from 1892 to 1957. (Photograph © Terry Donnelly)*

Above: *A spiral staircase winds to the top of the Presque Isle Lighthouse. (Photograph © Keith Baum/BaumsAway Stock Photography)*

Above: *Cars are not allowed on Mackinac Island, so residents and visitors must use other modes of transportation, such as bicycles and horse-drawn carriages. (Photograph © Layne Kennedy)*

Right: *Bicycles for rent are lined up to accommodate the many tourists that take the ferry to Mackinac Island each year. (Photograph © Layne Kennedy)*

Facing page: *Always charming, historic Mackinac Island tells the stories of a bygone era. (Photograph © Layne Kennedy)*

Facing page: *The Victorians first made Mackinac a popular resort spot, and many of the buildings on the island, like this bed and breakfast, reflect their influence. (Photograph © Keith Baum/ BaumsAway Stock Photography)*

Above: *Built in 1887, the Grand Hotel features the world's longest front porch, measuring 660 feet. (Photograph © Layne Kennedy)*

Left: *The prestigious Grand Hotel is abuzz with guests from May through October. (Photograph © Layne Kennedy)*

Left: *Mackinac Bridge, which crosses the Straits of Mackinac, is the only link between the Upper and Lower Peninsulas of Michigan. (Photograph © Doug Locke)*

Above: *At five miles across, the "Mighty Mac" is the third-longest bridge in the United States. (Photograph © Keith Baum/BaumsAway Stock Photography)*

Above: *While scores of people flock to Mackinac Island in the summertime, only five hundred residents live there through the winter. (Photograph © Layne Kennedy)*

Right: *When the weather gets cold, Mackinac Island elementary students must bundle up before venturing to school. (Photograph © Layne Kennedy)*

Snowmobiles are the vehicle of choice when wintertime comes to Mackinac Island. This snowmobiler is making a pizza delivery.
(Photograph © Layne Kennedy)

Facing page: *Hoar frost ices the trunks and leaves of these trees near Arch Rock. (Photograph © Layne Kennedy)*

Above: *The summer homes of Mackinac Island are quiet as shadows fall across a blanket of fresh snow. (Photograph © Layne Kennedy)*

Above: *The skeleton of a sunken ship rises from the waters of Lake Huron. (Photograph © Gary Alan Nelson)*

Right: *Sailboats float on the surface of Lake Huron, which surrounds Mackinac Island. (Photograph © Keith Baum/BaumsAway Stock Photography)*

Facing page: *Lake Huron is the third-largest of the Great Lakes and is connected to Lake Michigan by the Straits of Mackinac. (Photograph © Gary Alan Nelson)*

Facing page: *Water cascades over Bond Falls in the Upper Peninsula's Ottawa National Forest. (Photograph © Willard Clay)*

Above: *The rare Dwarf Lake Iris grows only in the Great Lakes region, with most of the flower's population lying within Michigan's borders. (Photograph © Doug Locke)*

Facing page: *The worn, wooden façade and remote location of East Channel Light, on Grand Island, make the 1870 lighthouse appear as though it's part of a ghost town. (Photograph © Layne Kennedy)*

Above: *Tombstones overgrown with moss mark the solitary graves of Cemetery Island, near Isle Royale National Park's Rock Harbor. (Photograph © Layne Kennedy)*

Left: *Red bunchberry, green bearberry, and mossy groundcover shroud the earth of the Upper Peninsula. (Photograph © Terry Donnelly)*

The city of Houghton, called the "Gateway to the Keweenaw Peninsula," is home to the Portage Lake Lift Bridge, the widest and heaviest double-decked vertical lift bridge in the world. (Photograph © Layne Kennedy)

Above: *At 165 feet long, the mighty Ranger III is the largest passenger ferry providing service to Isle Royale National Park. (Photograph © Layne Kennedy)*

Above: *Founded in 1688, Sault Ste. Marie is one of the oldest continuous settlements in the United States. The shipping industry has made the Soo Locks one of the world's most-used waterways. (Photograph © Keith Baum/BaumsAway Stock Photography)*

Well-used fishing nets await their next dip into the waters of Lake Superior. (Photograph © Layne Kennedy)

An experienced fisherman works at the restored Pete Edisen Fishery on Isle Royale National Park. (Photograph © Layne Kennedy)

Established as a National Park in 1940, Isle Royale is a popular getaway for anglers, hikers, and kayakers. (Photograph © Layne Kennedy)

Pictured Rocks was named the first National Lakeshore in 1966. The 70,000-acre park features many fascinating geological formations, such as Miner's Castle. (Photograph © Terry Donnelly)

Facing page: *Pictured Rocks National Lakeshore extends for forty miles along the Lake Superior coast. (Photograph © Willard Clay)*

Above: *Colored pebbles decorate the shoreline at Pictured Rocks. (Photograph © Gary Alan Nelson)*

Above: *Tannin from nearby cedar, spruce, and hemlock trees dyes Tahquamenon Falls an amber hue. (Photograph © Doug Locke)*

Right: *An early snow frosts the trees of the Copper Country State Forest. (Photograph © Gary Alan Nelson)*

Facing page: *At J. W. Wells State Park, plates of ice stack up on the shoreline of Lake Michigan. (Photograph © Gary Alan Nelson)*

Left: *This snowy owl has a bird's-eye-view from atop a telephone pole. (Photograph © Doug Locke)*

Leafless trees etch an intricate pattern into the snow and sky of a Michigan winter. (Photograph © Terry Donnelly)

Above: *Located on the Garden Peninsula at Snail Shell Harbor, Fayette State Historical Park was a busy industrial town until the Jackson Iron Company closed its Fayette smelting operation in 1891. (Photograph © Gary Alan Nelson)*

Left: *Cliffs Harbor is framed by the windows of an abandoned warehouse at Fayette State Park. (Photograph © Terry Donnelly)*

Facing page: *Cliffs overlook Big Bay de Noc at Fayette State Historical Park. (Photograph © Gary Alan Nelson)*

Above: *Mountain biking is one of many recreational activities that residents of Michigan enjoy. (Photograph © Layne Kennedy)*

Above: *Calypso orchids brighten the Upper Peninsula in springtime. (Photograph © Doug Locke)*

Facing page: *Pink clouds roll across the sky above the Tahquamenon River in Tahquamenon Falls State Park. (Photograph © Robert W. Domm)*

At Seul Choix Point, on the southern coast of the Upper Peninsula, sandstone boulders are encrusted with rust-colored lichen.
(Photograph © Gary Alan Nelson)

The mineral-painted sandstone cliffs of Pictured Rocks National Lakeshore tower 200 feet above Lake Superior. (Photograph © Gary Alan Nelson)

Facing page: *A mountain ash tree, heavy with brilliant red fruit, hangs over Miners River. (Photograph © Willard Clay)*

Left: *The Seney National Wildlife Refuge, in the Great Manistique Swamp, supplies more than 95,000 acres of inhabitable land for migratory birds and other wildlife. (Photograph © Gary Alan Nelson)*

Below: *Black bears, deer, coyotes, wolves, and moose are just some of the animals that roam Michigan's natural areas. (Photograph © Robert W. Domm)*

Left: *The Hiawatha National Forest, comprised of two units on Michigan's Upper Peninsula, touches three of the Great Lakes. (Photograph © Terry Donnelly)*

Above: *As summer turns to autumn, Chapel Falls cascades over a canyon wall in Pictured Rocks National Lakeshore. (Photograph © Terry Donnelly)*

Dawn breaks over Lake Superior and Isle Royale National Park. (Photograph © Gary Alan Nelson)